ANCIENT MYTHOLOGY

MAYA MYTHS AND LEGENDS

by Janie Havemeyer
illustrated by Cesar Samaniego

Tools for Parents & Teachers

Grasshopper Books enhance imagination and introduce the earliest readers to fun storylines and illustrations. The easy-to-read text supports early reading experiences with repetitive sentence patterns and sight words.

Before Reading

- Discuss the cover illustration. What do readers see?
- Look at the glossary together. Discuss the words.

During Reading

- "Walk" through the book with the reader. Discuss new or unfamiliar words. Sound them out together.
- Look at the illustrations. When and where does the story take place? What is happening in the story?

After Reading

- Prompt the child to think more. Ask: What is your favorite Maya legend? Why?

Grasshopper Books are published by Jump!
3500 American Blvd W, Suite 150
Bloomington, MN 55431
www.jumplibrary.com

Copyright © 2026 Jump! International copyright reserved in all countries. No part of this book may be reproduced in any form without written permission from the publisher.

Jump! is a division of FlutterBee Education Group.

Library of Congress Cataloging-in-Publication Data

Names: Havemeyer, Janie, author.
Samaniego, César, 1975- illustrator.
Title: Maya myths and legends / by Janie Havemeyer; illustrated by Cesar Samaniego.
Description: Minneapolis, MN: Jump!, Inc., [2026]
Series: Ancient mythology | Includes index.
Audience: Ages 7-10
Identifiers: LCCN 2024055463 (print)
LCCN 2024055464 (ebook)
ISBN 9798892137560 (hardcover)
ISBN 9798892137577 (paperback)
ISBN 9798892137584 (ebook)
Subjects: LCSH: Maya mythology–Juvenile literature.
Maya gods–Juvenile literature. | Mayas–Folklore–Juvenile literature.
Classification: LCC F1435.3.R3 H38 2026 (print)
LCC F1435.3.R3 (ebook)
DDC 355.02–dc23/eng/20250107
LC record available at https://lccn.loc.gov/2024055463
LC ebook record available at https://lccn.loc.gov/2024055464

Editor: Alyssa Sorenson
Direction and Layout: Anna Peterson
Illustrator: Cesar Samaniego
Content Consultants: Allen J. Christenson, PhD, Professor, Comparative Arts and Letters, Brigham Young University; Edwin Barnhart, PhD, Director of the Maya Exploration Center

Printed in the United States of America at Corporate Graphics in North Mankato, Minnesota.

Table of Contents

Maize and Magic	4
Maya Gods and Goddesses	22
To Learn More	23
Glossary	24
Index	24

Maize and Magic

In the beginning, Earth was covered in water. The sky touched it. Maya gods planted a tall tree. It pushed the sky up. It made room for life on Earth.

Huracan

The gods made the first people out of mud and wood. But these people could not **worship** them. Huracan, the sky god **creator**, sent a flood to carry them away. Next, the gods made humans out of **maize**. These humans honored the gods!

Many Maya live in North and Central America. They have told **legends** of goddesses and gods since **ancient** times. Maya legends explain how gods use their powers to change the world.

Once, the world was dark and cold. Humans went to the god Itzamná. He is the ruler of sky, day, and night. They asked him for light. He brought the Sun to the sky.

Other gods control weather. Once, it was hot and dry. **Crops** would not grow. Chaac is the god of rain and lightning. He threw his axe at a cloud. It cracked open. Rain poured out. Crops grew!

K'inich Ahau is the Sun god. Every day, he goes across the sky. He lights Earth with his bright rays.

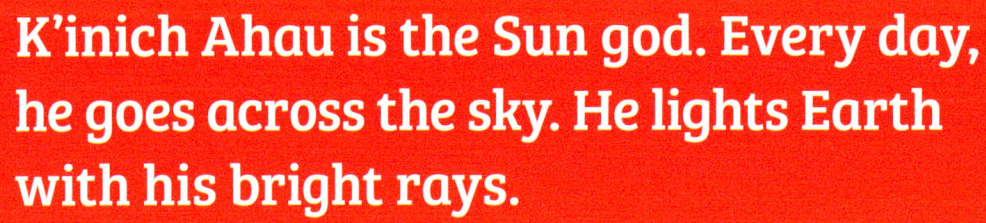

As the day goes on, K'inich Ahau grows older. By **dusk**, he has a beard and wrinkles. He is an old man.

At night, K'inich Ahau passes through the **underworld**. It is called Xibalba. Xibalba is very big. It takes 14 gods to rule it. It is not easy to leave. K'inich Ahau turns into a jaguar. He fights anything in his way.

K'inich Ahau's wife is Ix Chel. She is the Moon goddess. K'inich Ahau was not nice to her. Ix Chel ran away. Now, she only comes out at night, when K'inich Ahau is not there. The stars are her friends. Together, they light the night. This light guides travelers.

One Hunahpu was a good ball player. The underworld gods were jealous. They put his head in a tree.

Xquic was the daughter of an underworld god. She was pregnant with One Hunahpu's sons. She ran away to the surface.

Xmucane is One Hunahpu's mother. She is the goddess of childbirth. She tested Xquic. She told Xquic to fill a net with maize from one plant. It was impossible. But Xquic did it!

Xmucane

Xquic gave birth to twins. They were Hunahpu and Xbalanque. They were good ball players like their father. The underworld gods challenged them to a match. The twins won!

They took their father's head out of the tree. One Hunahpu became the maize god. He helps maize grow on Earth. People still eat it today!

Maya Gods and Goddesses

Who are the most important Maya gods and goddesses? Take a look!

Chaac
God of rain and lightning

Cizin
Ruler of Xibalba

Huracan
Sky god creator

Itzamná
Ruler of the sky, day, and night

Ix Chel
Moon goddess

K'inich Ahau
Sun god

Kukulkan
God of wind and storms

One Hunahpu
Maize god

Xmucane
Goddess of childbirth and mother of One Hunahpu

Xpiyacoc
God of marriage and father of One Hunahpu

To Learn More

Finding more information is as easy as 1, 2, 3.
❶ Go to www.factsurfer.com
❷ Enter "**Mayamythsandlegends**" into the search box.
❸ Choose your book to see a list of websites.

Glossary

ancient: Very old or from the very distant past.
creator: A person who creates, or makes, something.
crops: Plants grown for food.
dusk: The time of day after sunset when it starts getting dark.
legends: Stories handed down from earlier times.
maize: Corn.
underworld: A place in myths where the dead go.
worship: To show love and devotion to the gods.

Index

axe 8
Chaac 8
crops 8
flood 5
Hunahpu 19, 20
Huracan 5
Itzamná 6
Ix Chel 14

jaguar 12
K'inich Ahau 10, 11, 12, 14
maize 5, 18, 20
One Hunahpu 16, 18, 20
Xbalanque 19, 20
Xibalba 12
Xmucane 18
Xquic 16, 18, 19